MARRIAGE RIGHTS AND GAY RIGHTS

INTERPRETING THE CONSTITUTION

BARBARA GOTTFRIED HOLLANDER

ROSEN
PUBLISHING®

New York

Published in 2015 by The Rosen Publishing Group, Inc.
29 East 21st Street, New York, NY 10010

Copyright © 2015 by The Rosen Publishing Group, Inc.

First Edition

Library of Congress Cataloging-in-Publication Data

Hollander, Barbara Gottfried– author.
Marriage rights and gay rights: interpreting the Constitution/Barbara Gottfried Hollander.—First edition.
pages cm.—(Understanding the United States Constitution)
Includes bibliographical references and index.
ISBN 978-1-4777-7514-1 (library bound)
1. Same-sex marriage—Law and legislation—United States—Juvenile literature. I. Title.
KF539.H65 2014
346.7301'68--dc23

                                          2013043310

Manufactured in China

CONTENTS

INTRODUCTION

Marriage is the legal union between two people. By 2013, sixteen states and the District of Columbia had legalized marriage for both heterosexual and gay couples.

The date is June 25, 2013, and Americans are anxiously awaiting the Supreme Court's decision on marriage equality. At the heart of this decision is "What is marriage?" Until now, the country has answered with the Defense of Marriage Act (DOMA), which defines marriage as the union between a man and a woman. On this day, thousands of gay couples throughout the country cannot be married. They are denied more than one thousand rights already given to married couples of different genders. California even passed a state constitutional amendment called Proposition 8, which only recognizes marriages between the opposite sexes.

The date is now June 26, 2013. Today, the Supreme Court will decide on whether DOMA and Proposition 8 are constitutional. Will marriage continue to be defined in traditional terms? Or will the definition of marriage broaden to include gay men and lesbians? Facebook is home to many group postings about rallies and protests throughout the country: Do you support DOMA and Proposition 8? Join United for Marriage in Philadelphia. Are you in favor of marriage equality? View the Day of Decision Facebook page and unite with other supporters in San Francisco.

Hours pass and the Supreme Court hands down its ruling: the Defense of Marriage Act is unconstitutional. President Barack Obama commends the Court's decision to strike down "discrimination enshrined in law." A June 26, 2013, *USA Today* article cites the president's response: "The Supreme Court has righted that wrong, and our country is better off for it.…This ruling is a victory for couples who have long fought for equal treatment under the law; for children whose parents will now be recognized, rightly as legitimate; and for families that, at long last, will get the respect and protection they deserve; and for friends and supporters who have wanted nothing more than to see their loved ones treated fairly and have worked hard to persuade their nation to change for the better."

Minnesota representative Michele Bachmann has a different reaction. In a June 26, 2013, *Huffington Post* article, she says, "For thousands of years of recorded human history, no society has defended the legal standard of marriage as anything other than between man and woman. Only since 2000 have we seen a redefinition of this foundational unit of society in various nations. Today, the U.S. Supreme Court decided to join the trend, despite the clear will of the people's representatives through DOMA. What the Court has done will undermine the best interest of children and the best interests of the United States."

For over a decade, Americans have been divided on the issue of marriage equality. In August 2003, more than half of Americans opposed same-sex marriages, or marriages between two men or two women. In 2013, a *Washington Post*-ABC poll cited that 56 percent of Americans agreed with the Supreme Court decision that the Defense of Marriage Act was unconstitutional. Today, same-sex marriage is still debated in forums such as college campuses, online sites, and courtrooms. Many recent outcomes reflect an evolving definition of marriage and a changing American landscape.

CHAPTER ONE

THE RIGHTS OF MARRIAGE

s the word "marriage" mentioned in the U.S. Constitution? No. Did the original writers of this more than two-hundred-year-old document envision same-sex marriage? The 1971 *Baker v. Nelson* court case, as cited by the Minnesota State Legislature, answers, "It is unrealistic to think that the original draftsmen of our marriage statutes, which date from territorial days, would have used the term in any different sense. The term [same-sex marriage] is of contemporary [modern] significance."

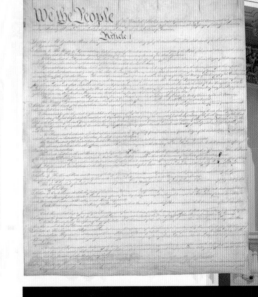

The U.S. Constitution was written in 1787. Each state also has its own constitution. A constitution describes the principles of the government.

CHANGE IT

While the original writers may not have envisioned same-sex marriage, they also did not legally support an end to slavery or voting rights for African Americans and women. These rights were granted in later constitutional amendments. Amendments are changes, deletions, or additions to the U.S. Constitution.

Article V of the U.S. Constitution outlines two steps for making an amendment:

1. Proposing: Introducing a change, deletion, or addition
2. Ratifying: Confirming and adopting the amendment

Lawmakers ratified the original U.S. Constitution in 1787. Since then, lawmakers have done the following:

- Introduced more than five thousand amendments
- Formally proposed thirty-three amendments
- Ratified twenty-seven amendments
- Repealed (or annulled) one amendment (the prohibition against alcohol)

The Thirteenth Amendment, which abolished slavery, was federally ratified in 1865. The Fifteenth

Amendment provided voting rights for African American men in 1870. And fifty years later, women were allowed to vote when the Nineteenth Amendment was ratified in 1920. Today, there is much discussion about affording gays and lesbians the same rights already given to heterosexual people (or people sexually attracted to those of the opposite sex).

GOVERNMENT BODIES

The U.S. Supreme Court was created in accordance with both Article III of the Constitution and the Judiciary Act. The U.S. Supreme Court consists of a chief justice and associate justices. Congress decides on the number of associate justices, which totaled eight in 2013. In August 2013, John G. Roberts Jr. was the chief justice of the U.S. Supreme Court, and its associate justices included Antonin Scalia,

In 1967, Thurgood Marshall became the first African American Supreme Court associate justice. When he retired in 1991, Associate Judge Clarence Thomas *(bottom row, left)* took his place.

Anthony M. Kennedy, Clarence Thomas, Ruth Bader Ginsburg, Stephen G. Breyer, Samuel A. Alito Jr., Sonia Sotomayor, and Elena Kagan.

- In 1993, Ruth Bader Ginsburg became the first Jewish woman to serve on the Supreme Court.
- In 2009, Sonia Sotomayor became the Supreme Court's first Hispanic justice and the third female justice.
- In 2010, Elena Kagan became the second Jewish woman to serve on the Supreme Court.

In its 221-year history, the U.S. Supreme Court has only had four female justices. Ginsburg, Sotomayor, and Kagan all ruled that the Defense of Marriage Act was unconstitutional.

The Supreme Court makes rulings (legally binding decisions made by a judge or group of judges) for lower U.S. courts to follow. These lower courts are found in all fifty states in the United States of America. Each state has its own court system, which includes a state supreme court. This means that states can pass different laws concerning the same issue. For example, one state may rule to allow only marriages between one man and one woman, while another state may rule to include gay marriages, too. States may also accept federal legal decisions on different schedules. It took Mississippi 149 more years than Nevada to ratify the amendment that bans slavery.

There are three branches of the U.S. government. The U.S. Supreme Court is part of the judiciary branch. Article 1 of the Constitution established the legislative branch of the U.S. government, which includes the House of Representatives and the Senate. Together, they form Congress, which has the power to enact legislation, or a group of laws. The legislative process includes the introduction and consideration of bills, or proposed laws. For example, the Respect for Marriage Act (RMA) is a bill that repeals DOMA and allows same-sex married couples to also enjoy benefits provided by the federal government.

WHAT IS MARRIAGE?

According to the online *Merriam-Webster Dictionary*, marriage has two definitions: "(1) the state of being united to a person of the opposite sex as husband or wife in a consensual and contractual relationship recognized by law (2) the state of being united to a person of the same sex in a relationship like that of a traditional marriage." What is the purpose of marriage? Is it companionship? Is it procreation (conceiving and bearing a child)? Many opponents of gay marriage believe that the main reason for marriage is to have children and argue that same-sex couples cannot procreate. But many gay and lesbian couples have found alternative ways, such as adoption and artificial insemination, to extend their families.

For same-sex marriage supporters, marriage rights are an important issue. There are over one thousand rights already given to married heterosexual couples. At the beginning of the twenty-first century, many of these same rights were denied to gay couples who resided in states that ban same-sex marriages, which meant the following:

1. Most gay men and lesbians were not entitled to excused time from work to care for their children or ill partners.
2. Most gay and lesbian couples were unable to have joint home and auto insurance plans.
3. Most gay and lesbian couples were not allowed to cover a partner on a health plan without paying taxes.
4. Most gay men and lesbians were denied participating in medical emergencies, like visiting their partners in the hospital. For example, in 2007, a woman named Lisa Pond collapsed during a vacation. Because of existing laws, her partner of seventeen years, Janice Langbehn, was not allowed to stay in Pond's hospital room or to

In October 2011, Janice Langbehn received the Presidential Citizens Medal for her efforts to promote equal treatment for all Americans.

obtain information about her condition. Langbehn was not even allowed to be with her partner when Pond died. President Obama responded by supporting regulation that called for an end to discrimination based on sexual orientation or gender identity.

5. Most gay and lesbian couples were ineligible for Medicaid or Medicare spousal protection.

Medicaid is a government program that provides free or low-cost health care for the needy; Medicare is a government program that gives health care for people aged sixty-five and older. Spousal protection provides the opportunity for a married person to keep part of his or her spouse's income for living expenses, like health care costs. If same-sex couples are not considered legally married, then they may not receive this assistance to pay bills.

6. Most gay and lesbian couples could not take out Social Security benefits (government benefits that provide money to people with little or no income) or to file wrongful death claims. These couples could also not take an excused personal work leave to mourn their partners' death or automatically inherit personal items (without a will).

7. Most gay and lesbian couples could not apply for residency or family unification through a spouse. For example, a gay man could not apply for a visa for his partner.

8. Most gay and lesbian couples were denied automatic rights to joint parenting, joint adoption, joint foster care, and visitation for nonbiological parents.

Jonathan Truong and Ed Cowen of New York adopted their son, Franklin. In 2013, there were sixteen states that allowed for gay couples to jointly petition for adoption.

9. Most gay and lesbian couples were not protected from testifying against each other in court.

10. Most gay and lesbian couples were not able to buy and own property under the same rules and protection as different-gender marriages.

11. Most gay and lesbian couples could not receive protective tax treatment for their retirement

plans. This reduces the amount of money available to pay bills.

12. Most gay and lesbian couples could not file joint tax returns and receive tax benefits related to marriage. The government gives certain financial tax benefits to married couples. Same-sex couples did not receive these same benefits because their marriages were not recognized.

INTERRACIAL AND SAME-SEX MARRIAGES

Same-sex marriage is often compared to interracial marriage, or the union between people of different races or ethnic groups. Prior to the U.S. Supreme Court case *Loving v. Virginia*, forty-one states banned marriage between an African American and a white person. Some states, like Virginia, also banned marriage between whites and other non-white groups like Asians. In 2013, forty-one states also banned same-sex marriage. Many opponents of interracial and same-sex marriages believe that allowing these marriages will encourage more of them, while supporters of interracial and same-sex marriages believe that marriage should extend beyond racial and gender limits.

Supporters of interracial marriage scored a victory with the 1967 U.S. Supreme Court landmark case *Loving v. Virginia*. The plaintiffs were Mildred Jeter Loving and Richard Perry Loving. They were an interracial couple who married in Washington, D.C., and wished to live as a married couple in Virginia. At that time, Virginia did not allow a Caucasian person and an African American to marry. In 1958, they were arrested for being in violation of the Racial Integrity Act.

The Lovings pleaded guilty and were allowed a suspension of their one-year sentence if they left Virginia and did not return as a married couple for twenty-five years. They moved to Washington, D.C., and eventually appealed their case in the U.S. Supreme Court. As reiterated in *Encyclopedia Virginia*'s *Loving v. Virginia* entry, the U.S. Supreme Court unanimously struck down the Virginia law, ruling that denying marriage based on race "is surely to deprive all the State's citizens of liberty without due process of law."

In 2003, Massachusetts's highest court cited two cases involving interracial marriage, *Loving v. Virginia* and *Perez v. Lippold*, in the same-sex marriage case *Goodridge v. Department of Public Health*, stating: "In this case [Goodridge], as in *Perez* and *Loving*, a statute deprives individuals of access to...the institution of marriage—because of a single trait: skin color in *Perez* and *Loving*, sexual orientation here. As it did in *Perez* and *Loving*, history must yield to a more fully developed understanding of the invidious quality of the discrimination." This ruling suggested that banning interracial and same-sex marriage was discriminatory.

IN THE BEGINNING...

In the 1971 case *Baker v. Nelson*, two
men, Jack Baker and Michael
McConnell, wanted to marry in
Minnesota. They filed an application
for a marriage license. But the men
were denied the license because they
were the same gender. Baker and
McConnell took their case to court,
arguing denial of due process and
equal protection under the U.S.
Constitution. At this time, the over-
whelming opinion was that
procreation (conceiving and bearing
children) was the purpose of marriage,
and same-sex couples could not procreate. While the court ruled that Jack
Baker and Michael McConnell were
not allowed to marry, it did not outlaw same-sex marriage.

Another 1970s same-sex court
case was *Jones v. Hallahan* in
Kentucky. In 1973, two women were
not allowed to obtain a marriage
license. They sued and claimed denial of three constitutional rights: the right to marry, the right to

Many same-sex couples rushed to marry before the Proposition 8 vote in California. This proposition was later overturned with the 2013 DOMA ruling.

associate, and the right to exercise their religion. As reiterated in Nolo's "Recognition of Same-Sex Relationships in Other States," the court held that "the relationship proposed does not authorize the issuance of a marriage license because what they propose is not a marriage." The definition of marriage between one man and one woman was upheld.

Several other 1970s court cases also upheld that marriage is the union between different genders:

- In 1974, the case *Singer v. Hara* appeared in the court system. In this case, a same-sex couple argued that denying same-sex marriage violated the Equal Rights Amendment.
- In a 1975 Ohio court case, *Thorton v. Timmers*, two lesbians were denied a marriage license when the court ruled that "it is the express legislative intent that those persons who may be joined in marriage must be of different sexes."
- In a 1975 Colorado case, *Adams v. Howerton*, an Australian citizen wanted to obtain U.S. residency through his American partner.

In all three cases, the court ruled against recognizing same-sex marriages. In the 1970s, there was no constitutional prohibition or protection regarding same-sex marriage.

CHAPTER TWO

AMEND IT

Marriage is not mentioned in the U.S. Constitution. However, both plaintiffs and defendants in same-sex court cases have cited different amendments when filing lawsuits. A plaintiff is the party that sues, and a defendant is the party that is being sued. For example, in *Loving v. Virginia*, Mildred Jeter Loving and Richard Perry Loving were the plaintiffs, and the State of Virginia was the defendant. As mentioned, an amendment is a change, deletion,

On June 12, 1967, the U.S. Supreme Court found in favor of Mildred and Richard Loving when they ruled to end all race-based legal restrictions on marriage.

or addition to the U.S. Constitution. There are several amendments that have been cited in same-sex cases, including the First, Fifth, Ninth, Tenth, and Fourteenth Amendments.

SEPARATION OF CHURCH AND STATE

According to the National Archives and Records Administration (NARA), the First Amendment of the Bill of Rights states: "Congress shall make no law respecting an establishment of religion, or prohibiting the free exercise thereof; or abridging the freedom of speech, or of the press; or the right of the people peaceably to assemble, and to petition the Government for a redress of grievances." How does this amendment affect same-sex marriage? Many opponents of same-sex marriage cite their religious beliefs to define marriage as the union between one man and one woman. In 2003, the Vatican (the Catholic papal government) along with Pope John Paul II launched a campaign against gay marriage.

In a twelve-page document cited in CNN.com's "Vatican Fights Gay Marriage," the Vatican stated, "Marriage exists solely between a man and woman ... Marriage is holy, while homosexual acts go against the natural moral law." The Vatican asked Roman

Catholic lawmakers to vote against legal- izing gay marriage and to repeal laws that granted rights to homosexual unions in Europe and North America. Another Vatican document also opposed the adop- tion of children by gay couples, stating, "Allowing children to be adopted by persons living in such [homosexual] unions would actu- ally mean doing violence to these children ... [placing] them in an environ- ment that is not conducive to their full human development."

Pope John Paul II criticized advancements for gay rights, such as same-sex marriage, in his 2005 book, *Memory and Identity*.

How did the Vatican react to the Supreme Court's DOMA decision that it was unconstitutional to define marriage as the union between one man and one woman? According to a *Newsmax* article, "Vatican's Top American: DOMA Decision Will Lead to Deaths," the U.S. Conference of Catholic Bishops called the DOMA decision "a tragic day for marriage and our nation." "The Court got it wrong," the bishops said. "The federal government ought to respect the truth that marriage is the union of one man and one woman, even where states fail to do so." Supporters of gay marriage often respond that the First Amendment prevents the implementation of a religious-based definition of marriage.

DOMESTIC PARTNERSHIP LAWS

Domestic partnership laws pertain to the rights of unmarried couples who live together like married couples, such as same-sex couples. These laws provide benefits to relationship partners. Many places do not have these laws. Therefore, if a same-sex couple moves from a place with domestic partnership laws to a place that does not recognize them, these rights are lost. By 2013, seven states and the District of Columbia had domestic partnership laws.

California was the first state to provide domestic partnership laws. In 1984, Berkley, California, became the first city to offer these laws to its employees. California has passed four legislative acts intended to provide same-sex couples with rights and responsibilities. In 1999, California allowed same-sex couples to have hospital visitation and state retirement health insurance coverage for dependents. In 2001, rights in California also included deciding medical issues, inheriting a partner's possessions without a will, using the state stepparent adoption process, and taking sick leave to care for a partner. In 2003, Assembly Bill 205 allowed domestic partners to benefit from most state-level marriage rights and responsibilities in California, beginning in January 2005.

Oregon and Washington provided same-sex couples with many state rights already given to heterosexual married couples. But these couples could still be denied federal rights. Maine, Hawaii, Nevada, and Wisconsin also provided specific domestic partnership laws. In 1982, Wisconsin became the first state to ban sexual orientation discrimination. In 2009, Washington, D.C., legalized same-sex marriages and recognized same-sex marriages performed in other states. In 2010, D.C. also allowed same-sex domestic partners to apply for marriage licenses free of charge.

IT'S ONLY FAIR

The Fifth Amendment of the Constitution deals with
being treated fairly when accused of a crime. The
NARA notes the exact text of the amendment: "No
person shall be held to answer for a capital, or other-
wise infamous crime, unless on a presentment or
indictment of a grand jury, except in cases arising in
the land or naval forces, or in the militia, when in
actual service in time of war or public danger; nor
shall any person be subject for the same offense to be
twice put in jeopardy of life or limb; nor shall be com-
pelled in any criminal case to be a witness against
himself, nor be deprived of life, liberty, or property,
without due process of law; nor shall private property
be taken for public use, without just compensation."

What does this mean and how does it relate to gay
marriage? The Fifth Amendment includes the guaran-
tee of due process. This process states that the
government must respect the rights, guarantees, and
protections of all citizens as given by the Constitution
(and its statues) before a person can be deprived of
life, liberty, and the pursuit of happiness. One of the
original writers of the U.S. Constitution, Thomas
Jefferson, referred to "life, liberty, and the pursuit of
happiness" as "inalienable rights," which are rights
that cannot be taken away, denied, or given to

SEC. OF STATE

T. JEFFERSON

President Thomas Jefferson thought the original U.S. Constitution
should include a Bill of Rights. The first ten amendments, including
the right to due process, were later added.

someone else. They are natural rights for all. Should marriage be a right for all, including both heterosexual and gay couples?

Within the legal system, two types of due process have evolved. Consider how they might apply to gay marriage:

- Procedural due process includes the rights to fair hearings, appropriate litigation, and jurisdiction to render judgment. This process has given same-sex couples the right to take legal action to try and obtain marriage licenses and other rights already given to different-sex marriages.
- Substantive due process means the government cannot intrude on the rights and liberties of individuals without being fair and reasonable. The 1986 court case *Bowers v. Hardwick* upheld laws that told gay couples how to behave sexually in the privacy of their own homes. The 2003 case *Lawrence v. Texas* overturned this ruling.

The 2013 Defense of Marriage Act ruling said that banning same-sex marriage is unconstitutional. Before this ruling, there were many legal rights denied to same-sex couples because they could not marry. This violated equal liberties afforded by the Fifth Amendment. The June 26, 2013, U.S. Supreme ruling stated, "DOMA's demonstrated purpose is to ensure that if any state decides to recognize same-sex marriages, those unions will be treated as second-class marriages for purposes of federal law. This raises a most serious question under the Constitution's Fifth Amendment." In addition to discriminating against same-sex couples, most of the U.S. Supreme Court justices also noted that DOMA "humiliates tens of thousands of children now being raised by same-sex couples." The full text for this ruling can be found at http://www.huffingtonpost.com/2013/06/26/defense-of-marriage-act-ruling_n_3454858.html.

STATE IT!

The Fifth Amendment applies due process at the federal level, while the Fourteenth Amendment involves due process at the state level. During the same-sex court case *Hollingsworth v. Perry*, U.S. Supreme Court Justice Antonin Scalia referred to both of these amendments. Later, when two men were accused of breaking a law because they engaged in sexual activity in the privacy of their own home, in *Lawrence v. Texas*, Judge Scalia again cited due process, saying that "liberty under the Due Process Clause gives them [same-sex couples] the full right to engage in [intimate] conduct without intervention of the government" (Cornell University Law School's Legal Information Institute). In the *New York Times*, Linda Greenhouse also quoted Justice Anthony M. Kennedy: "The state cannot demean their [gays] existence or control their destiny by making their private sexual conduct a crime."

In *Loving v. Virginia*, the defendants also stated that banning interracial marriage violated the equal protection and due process clauses of the Fourteenth Amendment. This amendment says that states cannot make or enforce laws that violate the privileges or immunities of American citizens or deprives them of life, liberty, or property, without due process. These clauses provide for equal protection under the law. In *Loving v. Virginia*, the U.S. Supreme Court ruled that banning marriage based on different races violated both of these clauses. The Bill of Rights Institute also cited the following from the U.S. Supreme Court ruling: "The freedom to marry has long been recognized as one of the vital personal rights essential to the orderly pursuit of happiness by free men.... To deny this fundamental freedom on so unsupportable a basis as the racial classifications…is surely to deprive all the State's citizens of liberty without due process of law."

A married couple, Kris and Lyssa White of Virginia, shows their support for gay marriage. Interracial marriage was once illegal in the United States, too.

If the freedom to marry is a "vital personal right," should this right be granted to all people? Supporters of gay marriage say yes. If this right is denied to same-sex couples, does it violate the U.S. Constitution? Supporters of gay marriage say yes again. And what about all the rights that are already given to opposite-sex married couples? Are gay married couples entitled to these rights, too? In 2013 the majority of U.S.

Proposition 8 plaintiffs Sandy Stier and Kris Perry speak at a press conference after the U.S. Supreme Court overturned the Defense of Marriage Act (DOMA).

Supreme Court justices ruled yes in the landmark DOMA decision.

IS IT RIGHT?

Same-sex court cases have also cited the Ninth and Tenth Amendments. The Ninth Amendment states, "The enumeration in the Constitution, of certain rights, shall not be construed to deny or disparage others retained by the people." This amendment refers to "unenumerated rights," which are assumed rights, such as the right to privacy. In 1986, Michael Hardwick was arrested for having sexual relations with another consenting man in his own home. Justice Byron White ruled that the right to privacy did not extend to sexual relations between individuals of the same sex. As discussed, this ruling was overturned seventeen years later by citing due process.

The Tenth Amendment deals with the freedom, independence, rights, and jurisdiction of the states. There is a balance of power between the federal and state governments. The U.S. Constitution mentions specific duties, such as declaring war and collecting taxes. The Tenth Amendment states that other duties are left to states and individuals. These have included domestic areas, such as issuing marriage licenses. A *Washington Post* article cites a Quinnipiac University

FULL FAITH AND CREDIT CLAUSE

The original writers of the U.S. Constitution wanted a unified country and included a full faith and credit clause. This clause requires states to recognize the legislative acts and decisions of other states. For example, Massachusetts recognizes legal name change contracts made in California. This clause also applies to things such as car registrations, divorces, adoptions, and heterosexual marriages. If a man and woman are married in one state, then this marriage is valid in all fifty states.

Yet, same-sex marriage has been treated differently. Some states allow same-sex marriages, while other states do not. This affects same-sex married couples who move between states. For example, in September 2013, Cara Palladino and Isabelle Barker moved from Massachusetts to Pennsylvania. They had wed in Massachusetts, where same-sex marriage had been legal since 2005. But they lost many rights when they moved to Pennsylvania, which did not allow same-sex marriage at that time. Denied rights included medical benefits and both parents' names on their son's birth certificate.

Many challenges confronted by same-sex couples were similar to those encountered by interracial couples several decades earlier. In the 1960s *Loving v. Virginia* case, the marriage between an African American woman and a Caucasian man was recognized in Washington, D.C., but considered illegal in

Virginia. In 2013, same-sex marriage was allowed in Washington, D.C., but not in Virginia. And if a same-sex couple was married in D.C., this union would not be recognized in Virginia. Justice Anthony Kennedy states in *Slate* that "no legitimate purpose overcomes the purpose and effect to disparage those whom the State, by its marriage laws, sought to protect in personhood and in dignity" regarding *United States v. Windsor*. Court cases, like the one filed by Cara Palladino and Isabelle Barker, can use this reasoning to argue that a state cannot refuse another state's legal decision to grant its citizens protection "in personhood and in dignity."

study that stated 56 percent of those polled believed that "same-sex marriage should be decided for all states on the basis of the Constitution. Just 36 percent said states should make the call."

In 2013, there was a state constitutional amendment from California called Proposition 8 that was decided on a federal level. This amendment defined marriage as the union between one man and one woman.

- In May 2008, the California Supreme Court ruled that same-sex couples have the right to marry. In November, Proposition 8 passed with 52 percent of the vote and overturned this ruling.

- In 2010, U.S. District Court judge Vaughn Walker declared Proposition 8 unconstitutional, claiming that it violated the Constitution's due process and equal protection clauses.

- In 2012, the Ninth Circuit Court of Appeals upheld Walker's ruling, citing that Proposition 8 "lessen[s] the status and human dignity of gay men and lesbians in California." Supporters of Proposition 8 reacted by taking their case to the federal level and asking the Supreme Court to decide.

- In 2013, the Supreme Court ruled that gay marriage is legal in California.

CHAPTER THREE

STATES RESPOND

Did the original writers of the U.S. Constitution envision that domestic issues (such as marriage, divorce, and adoption) would be under state jurisdiction? Many lawmakers and historians say yes. Yet, on September 21, 1996, the Defense of Marriage Act brought same-sex marriage into the federal arena. President Bill Clinton signed this bill, which banned federal recognition of same-sex marriage. This bill complicated things for state courts deciding same-sex marriage-related issues.

VERMONT PAVES THE WAY

In 1999 to 2000, the court case *Baker v. Vermont* paved the way for states to consider the rights, responsibilities, protections, and benefits denied to same-sex couples. The case began when three same-sex couples in Vermont

In November 1998, three gay couples challenged Vermont's marriage laws in the Vermont Supreme Court. In 2000, Vermont created civil unions for same-sex couples.

were denied the right to file for marriage licenses. Both the town and the state tried to dismiss the case, claiming that the purpose of marriage was to procreate. The Vermont Supreme Court ruled unanimously that denying same-sex marriage was unconstitutional. It also instructed the Vermont legislature to allow same-sex marriage or to provide similar rights for same-sex unions.

The Vermont Supreme Court ruling led the way for other states to consider the legality of same-sex marriages and the rights afforded to same-sex partners. On November 18, 2003, the Massachusetts

Supreme Court stated that the ban on same-sex marriages was unconstitutional. In 2004, four states tried to issue marriage licenses to same-sex couples:

- New Mexico issued twenty-six licenses, which the attorney general later made null and void.
- In San Francisco, California, almost four thousand same-sex couples also received marriage licenses. Less than a month later, the California Supreme Court ordered San Francisco to stop issuing these licenses.
- In New Paltz, New York, Mayor Jason West married same-sex couples but was later ordered to stop performing these ceremonies by the New York Ulster County Supreme Court.
- Oregon issued same-sex marriage licenses, which were rendered null and void about a year later.

In the first decade of the twenty-first century,

On February 27, 2004, Mayor Jason West married twenty-one same-sex couples. Major Jeffrey McGowan (*center*) and Billian Von Rostenberg (*right*) were the first to wed.

CIVIL UNIONS

Created by Vermont in 2000, civil unions are a state-granted legal status available for same-sex couples. A civil union allows spouses to benefit from legal protection at the state level. A civil union is different from a civil marriage. A civil marriage includes more than one thousand federal protections. It also comes with the respect and dignity that accompanies marital status.

Civil unions have other limitations. For example, they are most likely not transferable between states. This means that a same-sex civil union in Vermont will not be recognized in a state that does not allow same-sex marriage or civil unions. And when filling out forms that question marital status, civil union partners do not fit into any of the categories (such as married or single). Civil union partners are not even eligible for divorce.

Not including states that legalize marriage (where same-sex spouses enjoy state and federal rights and responsibilities), six states recognized civil unions for same-sex couples by June 2013. These states were Colorado, Delaware, Hawaii, Illinois, New Jersey, and Rhode Island. In 2009, Vermont became the fourth state to legalize gay marriage.

states were divided on the issue of same-sex marriage. In 2004, Arkansas, Georgia, Kentucky, Michigan, Mississippi, Montana, North Dakota, Ohio, Oklahoma, Oregon, and Utah constitutionally supported DOMA's definition of marriage as the union between one man and one woman. In 2005, Louisiana and Texas also had constitutional amendments that banned same-sex marriage. But that same year, the Massachusetts legislature rejected a constitutional amendment to ban same-sex marriage. The California legislature also legalized same-sex marriage, but then California governor Arnold Schwarzenegger vetoed the bill. In 2005, Connecticut upheld DOMA's marriage definition but also allowed civil unions.

Two thousand six was another pivotal year for same-sex marriage. Courts in Maryland and Georgia openly disagreed with a constitutional ban on marriage. Arizona rejected a constitutional ban on gay marriage, and New Jersey legalized civil unions. Yet, Alabama, Colorado, Idaho, South Carolina, South Dakota, Tennessee, Virginia, and Wisconsin all supported state constitutional amendments that banned same-sex marriage.

In 2008, the story changed again. Some decisions caused supporters of gay marriage to gain more ground. For example, the California Supreme Court ruled that a ban on same-sex marriage was

FIRST LEGAL SAME-SEX MARRIAGES

Same-sex marriage became legal in Massachusetts on Monday, May 17, 2004. On the Sunday night before this historical occasion, several of Massachusetts's cities and towns opened their offices in anticipation of handing out marriage licenses to same-sex couples. When the clock struck midnight, thousands of people began to cheer as city clerks distributed licenses. Marcia Hams and Susan Shepherd were the first in line to apply for their marriage license. Many couples followed and were greeted with thrown rice and the national anthem.

The year 2004 was an election year. Republican president George W. Bush and Democratic Massachusetts governor John Kerry both publicly opposed gay marriage, but they had different views on other same-sex related issues. For example, President Bush supported a constitutional amendment that banned gay marriage, while Governor Kerry supported civil unions for same-sex couples. At that time, many Americans did not support gay marriage. In fact, ballot questions that opposed gay marriage passed in eleven states. Much debate still exists about how gay marriage influenced voter turnout in the 2004 election.

unconstitutional, and the Connecticut Supreme Court ruled in favor of gay marriage. But opponents of gay marriage also scored victories when California passed Proposition 8 that banned same-sex marriage and both Florida and Arizona also passed state amendments to ban gay marriage.

Did you notice that decisions within the same state can significantly change over time? For example, in 2006, Arizona rejected a state constitutional ban on gay marriage. But in 2008, Arizona passed an amendment banning gay marriage. In 2005, the California legislature voted to legalize same-sex marriage. But in 2008, California passed a bill that defined marriage as between one man and one woman.

CALIFORNIA'S PROPOSITION 8

The California Marriage Protection Act, also known as Proposition 8, appeared on state ballots in 2008. If passed, this act would limit the definition of marriage to opposite sexes. It would also overturn the state's legalization of gay marriage. In anticipation of Proposition 8 passing, many gay couples rushed to get married in California before voting day. Some couples even traveled from other states. For example, a gay couple traveled from their home in Miami, Florida, to San Francisco for the opportunity to marry.

Proposition 8 was supported by organizations such as the Alliance Defense Fund. This Christian nonprofit group opposes gay marriage. ProtectMarriage.com is another proponent of marriage existing only between opposite sexes. This coalition includes California families, community leaders, religious leaders, and "pro-family organizations." It has a program called the Proposition 8 Legal Defense Fund. The Christian fundamentalist organization the American Family Association (an organization that supports Christian fundamentalist views) and the National Organization for Marriage (NOM) also supported Proposition 8.

Many organizations in support of gay marriage opposed Proposition 8, including the Human Rights Campaign, Marriage Equality, and Freedom to Marry. The Human Rights Campaign is a civil rights organization that strives for equality for lesbian, gay, bisexual, and transgender people. It calls for an expansion of the traditional definition of marriage to include same-sex couples. Marriage Equality is a grassroots organization that supports civil marriage equality, and Freedom to Marry is also dedicated to making marriage accessible to all couples.

Both supporters and opponents of Proposition 8 spent millions of dollars to promote their views. Following is a timeline for this controversial California law:

Proposition 8 supporters, who advocated outlawing same-sex marriage, cheered during a "Yes on 8 Bus Tour" stop at St. Frances X Cabrini Church in Los Angeles, California.

- On November 8, 2008, Proposition 8 passed with 52 percent of the vote.
- In May 2009, *Hollingsworth v. Perry* (also known as *Perry v. Schwarzenegger*) challenged Proposition 8 when two same-sex couples filed for marriage licenses. Judge Vaughn R. Walker allowed proponents to defend Proposition 8 and denied LAMDA Legal and cocounsel's request for lesbian, gay, bisexual (sexual attraction to both men and women), and transgender (identifying with a gender group other than one given at birth) groups to participate in the case.
- In 2010, Judge Walker ruled that Proposition 8 violated due process and equal protection. Proponents of Proposition 8 filed an appeal (request for a higher court to reverse a lower court's decision).
- In 2011, proponents legally requested that Judge Walker be removed from the case because he is gay. The U.S. District Court for the Northern District of California denied this motion, stating that a judge's sexual preference and personal relationships should not affect his participation in a case.
- In 2012, the Ninth Circuit declared Proposition 8 unconstitutional. Later that year,

the U.S. Supreme Court agreed to hear *Hollingsworth v. Perry.*

- In June 2013, as part of the DOMA ruling, the Supreme Court stated that proponents of Proposition 8 had no right to appeal. Same-sex supporters scored another victory.

Jeff Zarrillo *(left)* and Paul Katami, plaintiffs in California's Proposition 8 case, give a "thumbs up" to the U.S. Supreme Court's decision to strike down DOMA.

What were some of the reactions to the Proposition 8 ruling? The National Organization for Marriage's president, Brian Brown, stated, "Same-sex marriage in California is illegitimate, imposed by judicial activists in opposition to the expressed will of the people. The nation, and the rule of law, are worse for it." But the lead counsel for the *Hollingsworth v. Perry* case, David Boies, had a different reaction: "After years of unjust and unlawful discrimination, gay and lesbian Californians will no longer be treated as second-class citizens, unworthy of the fundamental right to marry the person they love.... Our Constitution guarantees liberty and equality for all, and today that promise was fulfilled for tens of thousands of gay and lesbian Californians and their families." Boies's reaction was reported in the June 26, 2013, press release, "VICTORY! Proposition 8 Is UNCONSTITUTIONAL for Good: Marriage Equality Returns to California."

CHAPTER FOUR

SAVE IT FOR COURT

Supporters and opponents of gay marriage have taken their stances from the streets to the courthouses. Many court cases in the second decade of the twenty-first century focused on Section 3 of the Defense of Marriage Act, which specifically states that marriage is between one man and one woman. Another key part of these cases involved was whose job it was to decide same-sex cases. Was it the job of the federal government? Or should these matters be left to the states, as the Constitution seems to suggest within the context of a federalist system of government?

ACTIVISTS IN SUPPORT OF AND OPPOSED TO GAY MARRIAGE

The 1969 Stonewall Riots were the beginning of the gay and lesbian civil rights movement.

On June 27, 1969, New York City police raided a gay Greenwich Village bar called the Stonewall Inn located on Christopher Street. Four nights of riots followed as gay men, lesbians, and transgender people fought back. Over the next few months, hundreds of people participated in protests as a show of support. One year after the riots, there was a Christopher Street Liberation Day. After the events, thousands of

People tried to stop the arrests of gay men and women during a 1969 police raid on the Stonewall Inn nightclub.

gays and lesbians participated in America's first gay pride parade.

Prior to December 1973, the board of the American Psychiatric Association listed homosexuality as a mental illness. On December 15, 1973, this listing was removed. One year later, the Ann Arbor, Michigan, City Council had its first openly gay American official, Kathy Kozachenko. In 1977, Dade County, Florida, stated that discrimination based on sexual orientation is illegal. Headed by singer Anita Bryant, a Christian fundamentalist group called Save Our Children fought this ordinance. A special election overturned the ordinance with 70 percent of the vote.

The year 1978 was a pivotal time for gay rights in California. The Briggs Initiative (also known as Proposition 6) called for the firing of any school employee who openly supported gay rights. Harvey Milk campaigned against the Briggs Initiative. Milk was the first openly gay public official in the United States. In 1977, he was elected to San Francisco's board of supervisors. In 1978, Milk was assassinated by Dan White, who was upset both by his recent job loss from San Francisco's City-County Board and by the growing tolerance for gay people. President Jimmy Carter and future president Ronald Reagan openly opposed the Briggs Initiative, which voters rejected by more than one million votes.

GAY CHARACTERS IN FILM AND TELEVISION

In 1967, a movie called *Guess Who's Coming to Dinner* depicted the announcement of an engagement between an African American man and a Caucasian woman. Actors and actresses, including Katherine Hepburn, Spencer Tracy, and Sidney Poitier, portrayed the reactions to this interracial relationship. The movie hit the screens in the same year as *Loving v. Virginia*. About twenty-five years later, the movie *Philadelphia* took on homosexuality, HIV/AIDS, and homophobia. And in 2005, almost twenty years later, the Academy Award–winning film *Brokeback Mountain* depicted the relationship between two gay men who were in love with one another but involved in heterosexual marriages.

Fast-forward another five years. Courts are ruling that Section 3 of DOMA is ruled unconstitutional. How did the entertainment world respond? According to Matt Kane, associate director of entertainment for GLAAD (Gay and Lesbian Alliance Against Defamation), "Film is in many ways quite behind the curve." Celebuzz.com also reported that GLAAD claims, "Of the 101 studio releases in 2012, only 14 contained LGBT [lesbian, gay, bisexual, and transgender] characters."

Yet, there have been some popular films and movies that include gay characters. Nominated for four Oscars, the 2010 film *The Kids Are All Right* tells the story of a lesbian couple who raises two children, one of whom seeks out his biological father. Other films with gay characters include *The Avengers*, *Ted*, and *American Reunion*. Award-winning TV shows, such as ABC's *Modern Family* and Fox's *Glee*, depict gay characters and their families. Opponents of same-sex marriage vocalized their opposition to the inclusion of gay characters. For example, in *USA Today*, Maria Puente quoted Bryan Fischer of the American Family Association, who felt that shows' and films' gay characters "desensitize the public to the raft of problems associated with homosexual behavior." The American Family Association supports marriage only between one man and one woman.

EXPANDING MARRIAGE DEFINITION AND RIGHTS

There were several landmark same-sex court cases that challenged the traditional definition of marriage and the exclusion of rights for same-sex couples. For example, the 1993 Hawaiian case *Baehr v. Miike* referred to same-sex exclusion as discrimination. In 1996, a judge in this case confirmed that same-sex couples were allowed to apply for marriage licenses. In response, same-sex opposition introduced the Defense of Marriage Act into state legislatures and the U.S. Congress. Eventually, DOMA passed at the federal level and legally defined marriage as the union between one man and one woman.

The 1996 case *Romer v. Evans* involved a state-wide proposal called Amendment 2, which prevented the Colorado state government from prohibiting discrimination based on sexual orientation. This meant that gays had minimal protection from discrimination in government workplaces. Romer was the governor of Colorado, and Evans was the plaintiff, who felt that Amendment 2 denied rights to gays. The U.S. Supreme Court ruled that Amendment 2 violated the equal protection clause of the Fourteenth Amendment and was unconstitutional.

In 2003, seven same-sex couples sued when they were denied marriage licenses by the Massachusetts Department of Health in the case *Goodridge v. Dept. of Public Health*. These same-sex couples had been in relationships ranging from seven to thirty-two years and wanted to legalize their unions as marriages. Some of these couples also had children. The couples wanted the same rights already given to heterosexual married couples. In a landmark ruling, the Massachusetts Supreme Judicial Court stated that denying same-sex marriage was unconstitutional. Massachusetts became the first state to legalize gay marriage. Connecticut followed as the second state. In 2009, the court case *Varnum v. Brien* resulted in Iowa becoming the third state to legalize same-sex marriage.

In 2004, Marcia Hams *(left)* and Susan Shepherd were the first same-sex couple to apply for a marriage license after gay marriage became legal in Massachusetts.

CHALLENGING DOMA

A few court cases have specifically challenged Section 3 of the Defense of Marriage Act. In 2010, *Gill v. Office of Personnel Management* claimed that DOMA violated the equal protection clause of the U.S. Constitution's Fifth Amendment because the act disrespects a group of people by denying them legal rights and responsibilities. This case also objected to marital decisions being made by the federal government, rather than the states. In 2010, district judge Joseph Tauro ruled that DOMA's Section 3 was in violation of the equal protection clause and same-sex marriage rulings were outside Congress's authority.

That year, *Gill v. Office of Personnel Management* was consolidated with *Commonwealth of Massachusetts v. United States Department of Health and Human Services*. In 2012, the U.S. Court of Appeals for the First Circuit ruled that Section 3 was unconstitutional in these cases. In 2012, the cases were asked to be heard again and eventually included in the 2013 landmark DOMA decision. The 2010 case, *Pedersen v. Office of Personal Management*, was similar to *Gill v. Office of Personnel Management*. In *Pedersen v. Office of Personal Management*, Judge Vanessa L. Bryant ruled that DOMA Section 3 was unconstitutional.

Section 3 of DOMA came under fire again in *Golinski v. Office of Personnel Management.* Lambda Legal is the largest national legal organization that supports civil rights for lesbians, gay men, bisexuals, transgender people, and those with HIV. In 2012, Lambda Legal filed a suit for Karen Golinski. She sued the Office of Personnel Management because she had been denied federal health benefits for her same-sex spouse. The case claimed that DOMA contradicted a federal appellate court's chief judge's prior ruling. In 2012, the District Court ruled that DOMA was unconstitutional. The Department of Justice asked to revisit the case, which was also included in the 2013 DOMA decision.

The 2010 *Dragovich v. U.S. Department of Treasury* court case was about California public employees who were not allowed to include their same-sex spouses on their health care and pension plans because of DOMA's Section 3. Federal judge Claudia Wilken of the Ninth Circuit ruled that Section 3 violates the equal protection rights and that California tax law unfairly denies same-sex couples access to the state's long-term care insurance plan. In 2011, a same-sex couple, Gene Balas and Carlos Morales, sued because they were denied the right to file for joint bankruptcy under DOMA. Judge Thomas Donovan was among twenty judges

Edith Windsor greeted supporters after leaving the U.S. Supreme Court in March 2013. Her case challenged the constitutionality of DOMA.

in the U.S. Bankruptcy Court of the Central District to rule that DOMA violated the Fifth Amendment's due process clause.

A key part of the June 26, 2013, DOMA ruling was the *Windsor v. United States* court case. Edie Windsor and her same-sex spouse, Thea Spyer, had been married in Canada and lived together for more than forty years in New York. When Spyer died, she willed her estate to Windsor. According to laws for married heterosexual couples (between one man and one woman), inheritances are not subject to federal taxes. Because this same tax benefit was not given to same-sex couples, Windsor was told to pay $363,000 in federal taxes. Her response was to sue the U.S. District Court for the Southern District of New York in November 2010. Again, the argument was that DOMA violated the equal protection clause of the U.S. Constitution.

By 2011, President Obama's administration had issued a memo that it no longer backed DOMA's Section 3 and cited *Windsor v. United States*. After this memo was issued, the House of Representatives' Bipartisan Legal Advisory Group (BLAG) reaffirmed their support of DOMA's Section 3 and the federal

President Obama greets Jonathan Hopkins at a Democratic National Committee Lesbian Gay Bisexual Transgender Leadership event. Hopkins is a former U.S. Army captain who was honorably discharged because of DADT.

ban on same-sex marriage. This group had tried to defend DOMA in cases, such as *Gill v. Office of Personnel Management*, *Commonwealth of Massachusetts v. United States Department of Health and Human Services*, and *Windsor v. United States*. In 2012, the U.S. Court of Appeals for the Second Circuit in New York reaffirmed that DOMA's Section 3 was unconstitutional. On June 26, 2013, the Supreme Court officially upheld this ruling.

LAW OF DON'T ASK, DON'T TELL

Don't Ask, Don't Tell (DADT) was a law that was passed by Congress in 1993. It mandated that openly gay, lesbian, and bisexual people be discharged from the army. DADT resulted in over 14,500 service members being fired from the armed services because they did not hide their sexual orientation. Signed by President Clinton, DADT stated that the presence of gay people in the armed services "would create an unacceptable risk to the high standards of morale, good order and discipline, and unit cohesion which are the essence of military capability." This law was based on the U.S. Supreme Court ruling in *Bowers v. Hardwick*, the text of which can be found in the Congressional Research Service's article "'Don't Ask, Don't Tell': The Law and Military Policy on Same-Sex Behavior."

Margaret Witt was discharged from the air force for being gay. In September 2010, a federal judge gave her the option of returning to military service.

But *Bowers v. Hardwick*, which dictated the sexual behavior of gays in the privacy of their own homes, was overturned with *Lawrence v. Texas* in 2003. In 2004 DADT was challenged in court with *Log Cabin Republicans v. United States*. Later, in 2006, Major Margaret Witt was discharged after serving for eighteen years in the air force because it was alleged that she had sexual activity with a female civilian with whom she shared a relationship. The American Civil Liberties Union (ACLU) sued, claiming a violation of liberty and equal protection.

In September 2010, the Federal District Court ruled that the government failed to show cause for Witt's discharge and ordered that she be allowed to resume her service. In 2010, the U.S. District Court also ruled that DADT was unconstitutional and banned enforcement of this law. In May 2011, Witt's lawsuit was settled. She retired with full benefits and the unlawful discharge was removed from her record. The government also agreed not to appeal.

Two thousand ten was a pivotal year for gays serving in the armed forces. A CNN poll taken on November 17, 2010, showed that 72 percent of Americans supported repealing (or formally withdrawing) DADT. A 2009 Gallup poll even noted that the majority of conservatives and churchgoers supported repealing the law. In May 2010, the House of Representatives adopted a National Defense Authorization Act Amendment that supported DADT's repeal. On December 15, 2010, the House passed a bill to support DADT's repeal, and three days later, the Senate passed a similar bill.

On December 22, 2010, President Obama signed a bill to repeal DADT. The repeal of this law went into effect on October 20, 2011. A U.S. Department of Defense article by Jim Garamone quotes Defense Secretary Leon. E. Panetta as stating, "All men and woman who serve this nation in uniform—no matter their race, color, creed, religion, or sexual orientation—do so with great dignity, bravery, and dedication…They put their lives on the line for America, and that's what really matters. Thanks to

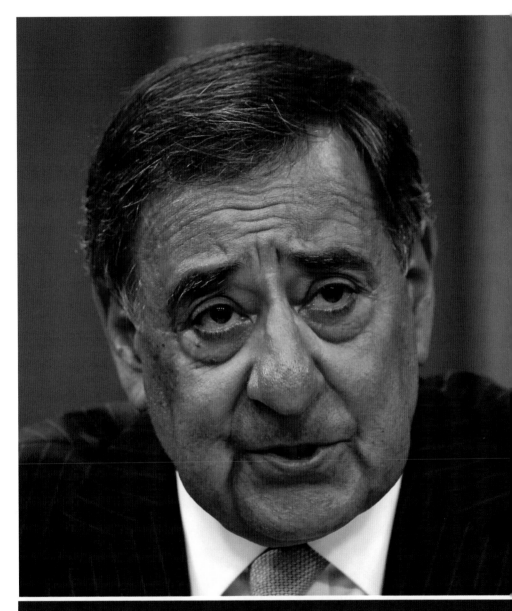

In 2013, Defense Secretary Leon E. Panetta stated that discrimination based on sexual orientation would no longer be tolerated in the Department of Defense.

the professionalism and leadership of the U.S. military, we are closer to achieving the goal that is at the foundation of America—equality and dignity for all." One effect of the repeal was that gay soldiers openly embraced their sexual orientation and turned "don't tell" into "do tell." For example, twenty-one-year-old U.S. Air Force soldier Randy Phillips announced his homosexuality to his father with a YouTube video that had almost seven million hits as of October 2013, according to James Nichols in the *Huffington Post*.

Even with the repeal of DADT in 2011, same-sex military couples were still denied certain spousal rights because of the Defense of Marriage Act. Even after DOMA was ruled unconstitutional, some gay military couples still faced challenges from organizations. For example, the Southern Baptist Convention's North American Mission Board prohibited Baptist chaplains from supporting, performing, or even attending gay marriage ceremonies either on or off army bases. Yet, the first academic study of an open-service policy toward people of all sexual orientations confirmed that there were no negative consequences of repealing DADT.

Since the repeal of DADT and the June 2013 DOMA ruling, the federal government has extended many rights to same-sex military couples. In fact, in August 2013, the Department of Justice announced that same-sex spouses of military employees are eligible for the same benefits as heterosexual military spouses. Benefits include traveling to a state offering same-sex marriage legalization for the purpose of getting married. For example, in 2011, gay marriage was legal in Vermont, but not Arizona. Navy lieutenant Gary Ross and his partner Dan Swezy traveled from Arizona to Vermont to wed. Other benefits include hospital visitation and the right to file for domestic partnership status, which adds twenty-two more benefits.

Equal rights also includes fair pay

In June 2013, U.S. Air Force Senior Airman Shyla Smith (left) and Courtney Burdeshaw were ready to wed in New York.

because salary is partly dependent on marital status. Gay military couples were also eligible for benefits, such as services that help families cope with long-distance relationships for prolonged periods of time. OutServe-SLDN specifically serves and supports LGBT (lesbian, gay, bisexual, and transgender) military personnel and their families and encourages an inclusive military environment. One year before DOMA was ruled unconstitutional, the Pentagon hosted its first gay pride celebration for U.S. troops.

CHAPTER FIVE

TO THE FUTURE

The gay marriage landscape has changed significantly in the twenty-first century. More states are considering same-sex marriage legalization. They are also considering other same-sex related issues, such as the status of same-sex marriages across state lines and the inclusion of more rights, benefits, and protections for same-sex couples. Many Americans are becoming more accepting and aware of same-sex relationships, and many gay men and lesbians are more comfortable expressing their sexual orientation. For example, in 1986, there were no openly gay law clerks in the U.S. Supreme Court. But in January 2013, thirty members of the LGBT Bar Association (once known as the National Lesbian and Gay Law Association) were admitted to the U.S. Supreme Court's Bar.

America's position on same-sex marriage is still open for debate. There are many groups that support and oppose gay marriage. For example, Generation Y (those born from the 1980s to early 2000s) is three times as likely to support gay marriage than oppose it. Republicans are two-and-a-half times more likely to oppose gay marriage than support it, however, and people who attend church weekly are also twice as likely to oppose it than non-regular churchgoers. In 2003, the Vatican with Pope John Paul II launched an antigay marriage campaign. In 2013, recently appointed Pope Francis reaffirmed the Catholic Church's position against homosexuality but also stressed "respect and compassion" for lesbians, gays, bisexuals, and transgender people. So what does the future hold for same-sex marriage?

RESPECT FOR MARRIAGE ACT BILL

Representatives Bob Barr from Georgia and Don Nickles from Oklahoma originally introduced the Defense of Marriage Act. The intent was to define marriage at the federal level as the union between opposite sexes. DOMA passed in both the House of Representatives and the Senate, and President Bill Clinton signed the bill in 1996. Fifteen years later, the Obama administration supported repealing DOMA and asked that the Department of Justice not defend it.

On June 26, 2013, the Respect for Marriage Act was introduced into the House of Representatives as a replacement for the Defense of Marriage Act. The Respect for Marriage Act calls for states to issue marriage licenses, which in turn will be respected by the federal government. For example, this means that the federal government would respect marriage licenses given to same-sex couples in California. This also

In 2013, supporters of marriage equality rallied in favor of legalizing same-sex marriage. Several months later, the U.S. Supreme Court ruled that DOMA was unconstitutional.

means that same-sex spouses in California would enjoy the same federal rights, protections, and benefits as heterosexual spouses.

Although the act calls for states to issue marriage licenses, it does not require states to legalize same-sex marriages or force anyone to perform a same-sex marriage or grant licenses to same-sex couples. So, how did Americans weigh in on same-sex marriage before the introduction of this bill? A 2008 *Newsweek/* Princeton Research survey reported that 70 percent of Americans already believed that same-sex couples should have certain rights and benefits given to heterosexual married couples, such as Social Security and insurance benefits and hospital visitation rights. A 2011 HRC/Greenberg Quinlan Rosner Research survey also showed that the majority of people in the United States support nullifying DOMA.

CONVERSION THERAPY

Conversion therapy (also known as reparative or reorientation therapy) attempts to change a person's sexual orientation. For example, conversion therapy has been used to try and "change" a gay man to a heterosexual man. It is based on the idea that people can change their sexual attractions, rather than accept and respect people's existing sexual preferences. Patients of conversion therapy have reported increased depression and anxiety, mental breakdowns, and suicidal thoughts. Some shared that they feel like failures because their therapy sessions attempt to change who they are and equate no change with lack of effort.

As documented by the Human Rights Campaign in "The Lies and Dangers of Efforts to Change Sexual Orientation or Gender Identity," many medical organizations have criticized conversion therapy, such as some of the following:

- American Academy of Pediatrics: "Therapy directed specifically at changing sexual orientation is contraindicated, since it can provoke guilt and anxiety while having little or no potential for achieving changes in orientation."
- American Medical Association: "Our AMA opposes the use of 'reparative' or 'conversion' therapy that is based on the assumption that homosexuality per se is a mental disorder or based upon the a priori assumption that the patient should change his/her homosexual orientation."
- National Association of Social Workers' National Committee on Lesbian, Gay and Bisexual Issues (NCLGB): "Aligned with the

American Psychological Association's (1997) position, NCLGB believes that such treatment [conversion therapies] potentially can lead to severe emotional damage. Specifically, transformational ministries are fueled by stigmatization of lesbians and gay men, which in turn produces the social climate that pressures some people to seek change in sexual orientation. No data demonstrate that reparative or conversion therapies are effective, and in fact they may be harmful."

How have states responded to the issue of conversion therapy? California was the first state to ban conversion therapy for minors (under the age of eighteen). But this ban came under fire from therapists and families who responded with lawsuits. They claimed that the ban violated the First Amendment because it interfered with free speech rights between therapists and patients (and their parents) who might want to discuss "gay conversion." In August 2013, the Ninth U.S. Circuit Court of Appeals unanimously agreed that the ban did not violate free speech. The defendants (those opposing the ban) planned to appeal.

In 2013, New Jersey governor Chris Christie signed a bill that banned conversion therapy, making New Jersey the second state to ban this treatment. The

Michael Ferguson *(second from right)* and three other gay men accused a New Jersey organization of subjecting them to various humiliations under the guise of "conversion therapy," which promised to make them straight.

bill prevents licensed therapists, psychologists, social workers, and counselors from trying to convince gay teenagers to become straight. Liberty Counsel is a national religious-based legal and public policy group that challenged the California ban. It also legally challenged the New Jersey ban on behalf of the therapists and two associations. Liberty Counsel again claimed that the ban violated the First Amendment and prohibited New Jersey licensed therapists from respecting clients' rights for sexual orientation counseling.

In August 2013, Pennsylvania introduced bills to ban gay conversion therapy. The Liberty Counsel became involved again, citing that the ban violates both the First and Fourteenth Amendments. Pennsylvania representatives Brian Sims and Gerald Mullery sponsored the bill. In "Sims, Mullery to Introduce Ban on Anti-Gay 'Conversion Therapy' for Minors" from the Pennsylvania House of Representatives," Mullery stated, "When I became aware of what was involved in conversion therapy, I equated it to medical and parental bullying. Children who were subjected to this so-called therapy suffer the same effects as children who were subjected to traditional bullying, including suicide, attempted suicide, and low self-esteem." In 2013, Massachusetts and New York were also considering introducing bills to ban conversion therapy.

"SAME LOVE"

The popular song "Same Love" by Macklemore and Ryan Lewis provides a response to the belief that gay people can change their sexual orientation:

And I can't change
Even if I tried
Even if I wanted to
And I can't change
Even if I tried
Even if I wanted to
My love, my love, my love
She keeps me warm.

Originally, Macklemore (also known as Ben Haggerty) wanted to write a song to support gay rights and marriage equality and to combat homophobia (fear or hatred of gay men and lesbians). "Same Love," co-written and directed by Macklemore and Lewis, was released on July 18, 2012. The song was created to support marriage equality and a bill that would legalize gay marriage in Macklemore's home state of Washington.

On October 2, 2012, the "Same Love" video posted and received 350,000 hits in 24 hours. On October 20, 2012, the duo performed the song with Mary Lambert on *Ellen*. Called the gay equality anthem, "Same Love" made it to number nine on the Billboard Top 20. It became even more popular after the June 2013 DOMA decision. As reported by Sarah Muller, after he and Lewis won at the Video Music Awards in August 2013, Macklemore stated, "Gay rights are human rights; there is no separation."

STATES' POSITIONS IN 2013

In December 2013, sixteen states and the District of Columbia (D.C.) had legalized marriage. These legalizations took place by court decision, state legislature (such as constitutional amendment or state law), or popular vote (election-based). Five of these states legalized gay marriage by court decision: New Jersey, Massachusetts, Connecticut, Iowa, and California. Eight states legalized gay marriage through state legislation: Vermont, New Hampshire, New York, Delaware, Minnesota, Rhode Island, Illinois and Hawaii. Maine, Maryland, and the District of Columbia legalized gay marriage by popular vote.

By contrast, in September 2013, thirty-five states banned same-sex marriages. Of these states, twenty-five issued this ban after DOMA passed in 1996. The following states banned gay marriage by both constitutional amendment and state law: Alabama, Alaska, Arizona, Arkansas, Colorado, Florida, Georgia, Hawaii, Idaho, Kansas, Kentucky, Louisiana, Michigan, Mississippi, Missouri, Montana, North Carolina, North Dakota, Ohio, Oklahoma, South Carolina, South Dakota, Tennessee, Texas, Utah, Virginia, and Wisconsin. Three states banned gay marriage only by a state amendment: Nebraska, Nevada, and Oregon. Five states used state law: Illinois,

Pennsylvania, Indiana, West Virginia, and Wyoming. Some states that ban gay marriage still recognize domestic partnerships and civil union laws. Only New Mexico did not legalize or ban gay marriage.

In a February 2013 Policymic article, Ned Flaherty wrote that Illinois, Hawaii, Michigan, Oregon, Colorado, New Mexico, and Nevada were among the next possible states to legalize gay marriage. These states had pro–same-sex marriage issues evolving throughout the rest of 2013. For example, Lambda Legal and the American Civil Liberties Union represented twenty-five same-sex couples in a lawsuit in Illinois. In September, Hawaiian governor Neil Abercrombie called for a special legislative session to legalize gay marriage. That same month, the Portland (Oregon) Business Alliance supported amending the state constitution to allow for gay marriage. By December 2013, both Illinois and Hawaii had legalized gay marriage.

GAY MARRIAGE RIGHTS IN THE TWENTY-FIRST CENTURY

From repealing Don't Ask, Don't Tell to instructing the Department of Justice not to back DOMA, the Obama administration has been a proponent of same-sex couples.

The U.S. Supreme Court's June 2013 DOMA decision meant that the federal government must give legally married same-sex couples the same benefits as heterosexual ones, including Social Security and tax benefits. Even before this ruling, in 2010, President Obama had already instructed most hospitals (those receiving Medicaid or Medicare funds) to allow for visitation of same-sex partners.

Following the 2013 DOMA ruling, the Obama administration tried to make federal benefits more accessible to same-sex married couples. This meant reforming more than one thousand laws from taxes to insurance. For example, same-sex spouses could receive their partner's health insurance and retirement funds. The Social Security Administration paid out retirement benefits to same-sex spouses. At this time, the Department of Homeland Security also gave gay married couples the same treatment under immigration law as opposite-sex married couples.

Gay married couples were also potentially eligible for other rights and benefits already given to heterosexual married couples. These rights included filing for bankruptcy (a process that helps debtors, or people who owe money, start over financially) and taking part in the Family Medical Leave Act, which provides benefits such as twelve weeks of unpaid leave within a year to care for medically ill spouses. Even filing for college financial aid was affected by marital status because it requires the income and contributions of parents. Prior to the June 2013 DOMA ruling, only one gay parent could be included on a student's financial aid application.

Adoption has also been challenging for same-sex couples, who often faced discrimination from adoption agencies. This included favoring opposite-sex couples and denying adoption based on "moral or religious grounds." Florida even had a law that banned same-sex couples from adopting children. Being denied the right to extend the family unit has many negative emotional consequences. It also has financial ones. The amount of federal taxes owed partially depends on family size. In the Family Equality Council's All Children Matter report, the council reported that a family of four with same-sex parents paid almost $5,500 more in taxes than the family with heterosexual parents.

But all this changed in 2013, when same-sex married couples were allowed to file taxes jointly. Joint filing affected income, gift, and estate taxes; income tax deductions; employee benefits; and contributions to government-sponsored retirement funds. These rights apply only to gay married couples—not domestic partnerships or civil unions. In 2013, most states did not recognize same-sex marriages. Yet, the federal government expanded the rights available to same-sex married couples and even mandated how hospitals

TEENS
SPEAK OUT

Gay marriage is a popular topic for all ages. In 2009, about sixty-five thousand children lived with gay parents. In the Family Equality Council's Voices of Children, Brian Arsenault wrote about how it felt to be raised in a family with two mothers. He was also aware of the difference in rights given to same-sex couples, like his parents: "My parents—my two moms—go to work every day, like other parents. They cook dinner and mow the yard. They take care of the house. Volunteer in the community. Pay their bills. Do the thousands of little things that keep a household running. And they love me, unconditionally. But it didn't take me long to realize that my mom and her partner didn't have the same rights as other people. They are treated differently by the law and can't do many of the things that other families take for granted."

Teens with heterosexual parents have also spoken out on both sides of the gay marriage issue. Factors that may influence the viewpoints of teens on same-sex marriage include degree of religious observance and location (such as residing in a state that legalized gay marriage). There are many forums, particularly online, where teens can voice their opinions on same-sex marriage. Overall, America's youth has grown in its support for marriage equality.

Bullying gay people, including gay teens, continues to be an issue despite the increase in rights given to same-sex married couples. Gay teens are more likely to be bullied than heterosexual ones. According to Bullying Statistics (www.bullyingstatistics.org), 30 percent of gay students who commit suicide suffer from sexual identity crises. The Violence Prevention Works site, http://www.violencepreventionworks.org, reported that 93 percent of teens have heard derogatory comments at least once about a person's sexual orientation.

U.S. News and World Report found that one in every seven teens were bullying targets because they were thought to be gay. Programs such as Safe Zone strive to increase the safety of students in school settings. With the ruling of DOMA as unconstitutional, many proponents of gay marriage hope that increased acceptance and equal rights will decrease the discrimination against gays found in many schools across the country. Gay teens looking for an online resource that seeks to provide hope for gays, lesbians, bisexuals, and transgender youth can visit www.itgetsbetter.org.

receiving government funds could treat hospital visitation by same-sex partners. The ruling that DOMA was unconstitutional removed the responsibility of defining marriage from the federal level. It also allowed for the federal government to offer many rights to both gay and heterosexual married couples.

On August 4, 2010, same-sex couple Maria Ydil *(left)* and Vanessa Judicpa waited for the ruling on Proposition 8. This measure denied gay couples the right to marry in California.

SAME-SEX MARRIAGE AROUND THE WORLD

According to the Pew Research Religion & Public Life Project (updated July 16, 2013), more than a dozen countries in the world have legalized gay marriage. Not all countries that legalized gay marriage provide the same legal protections, rights, and benefits for all married couples. For example, some countries legalized gay marriage but do not provide the right for same-sex couples to adopt children. Yet, in these same countries, opposite-sex married couples have the right to adopt. Same-sex marriage around the globe began with the Netherlands:

Country	Date That Same-Sex Marriage Was Legalized	Details
The Netherlands	December 2000	The Netherlands became the first country to legalize gay marriage.
Belgium	January 2003	Gay couples were also granted the right to adopt children in 2006.
Canada	2005	Gay couples received most of the legal marriage benefits by 1999.
Spain	2005	Spain ruled for marriage equality.
South Africa	November 2006	Civil officers and religious institutions cannot be forced to perform gay marriage.
Norway	January 2009	Same-sex couples can both marry and adopt children.
Sweden	April 2009	Civil unions for gay couples allowed since 1995.
Iceland	June 2010	One of the first same-sex marriages in Iceland was between the country's prime minister, Johanna Sigurdardottir, and her partner, Jonina Leosdottir.
Portugal	June 2010	Law does not allow married gay couples to adopt children.
Argentina	June 2010	Argentina became the first Latin American country to legalize gay marriage.

Denmark	June 2012	Queen Margrethe II gave her royal assent.
Uruguay	May 2013	The country has allowed civil unions for same-sex couples since 2008 and granted adoption rights for gay men and lesbians in 2009.
France	May 2013	French President Francois Hollande signed a law that legalized gay marriage.
Brazil	May 2013	The country's National Council of Justice ruled that marriage licenses cannot be denied to same-sex couples.
England and Wales	July 2013	In July 2013, the bill to legalize same-sex marriage received a "royal assent" from Queen Elizabeth II. Scotland and Northern Ireland were not included because they have separate legislative bodies to rule on issues such as same-sex marriage.
New Zealand	August 2013	The country was the first in the Asia-Pacific region to allow same-sex marriages.

In 2013, there were also countries with regional freedom to marry, where same-sex marriage was legal in certain parts of the country. These countries include the United States, where same-sex marriage was legal in sixteen states and the District of Columbia; Mexico, where same-sex marriage was legal in Mexico City and Quintana Roo; and Australia, where the nation's capital became the first territory to legalize gay marriage. In 2013, Columbia was also cited as a country that might soon legalize marriage.

Finally, there were countries that provided rights, but not legalized marriage, to same-sex couples in 2013. Many rights were given to same-sex couples in Ecuador, Finland, Germany, Greenland, Hungary, Ireland, Sweden, and Scotland. Countries that offered some rights included Andorra, Austria, Colombia, Croatia, Czech Republic, Liechtenstein, Luxembourg, Slovenia, and Switzerland. Israel also recognized gay marriages that took place in other countries.

FULL CIRCLE

In 1969, the Stonewall Riots launched a civil rights movement for gays and lesbians. In 2013, almost half of the states that recognized same-sex marriage legalized them that year. One-third of countries that recognized same-sex marriage also made

Six months after gay marriage became legal in Maryland, same-sex couple Sherrette Estes *(left)* and Maribel Garate shared a kiss at their wedding reception in Rockville, Maryland.

them legal in 2013. David Von Drehle wrote on Time.com that "the gay and lesbian community has gone from Stonewall to the altar in two generations."

Upon hearing that she won the landmark DOMA case on June 26, 2013, Edie Windsor also referred to Stonewall, where it all began. "I wanna go to Stonewall right now," she told the *New Yorker*. Windsor's case against the Defense of Marriage Act started when she received a $363,000 estate tax bill after her wife, Thea Spyer, passed away. Windsor remarked that if her spouse was "Theo" instead of "Thea," she would not have received the bill.

As shared in NBCNews.com's "'I Cried, I Cried': DOMA Widow Says on Hearing of Supreme Court Win," the decision that DOMA was unconstitutional brought tears to Windsor's eyes. "Children born today will grow up in a world without DOMA. And those same children who happen to be gay will be free to love and get married—as Thea and I did—but with the same federal benefits, protections and dignity as everyone else," said Windsor. "If I had to survive Thea, what a glorious way to do it and she would be so pleased."

GLOSSARY

amendment A change, deletion, or addition to the U.S. Constitution.

appeal A request for a higher court to reverse a lower court's decision.

bill A proposed law.

bisexual Sexually attracted to both men and women.

civil union A legal same-sex relationship that yields some of the rights and responsibilities of opposite-sex marriages.

Defense of Marriage Act (DOMA) A federal law that defined marriage as the union between one man and one woman.

discrimination Unfair treatment of a person based on prejudice.

due process When the government respects the rights, guarantees, and protections of all citizens as given by the Constitution (and its statues) before a person can be deprived of life, liberty, and the pursuit of happiness.

gay Sexually attracted to a person of the same sex (or gender).

gay marriage Marriage between two women or two men; also known as same-sex marriage.

gender State of being male or female.

heterosexual Sexually attracted to a person of the opposite sex (or gender).

homosexual Sexually attracted to a person of the same sex (gender).

lesbian Gay (homosexual) woman.

plaintiff The party that sues.

procreation Conceiving and bearing children.

repeal To make null and void.

ruling A legally binding decision made by a judge or group of judges.

transgender Identifying with a gender group other than one given at birth.

U.S. Supreme Court The highest judicial court in the United States.

FOR MORE INFORMATION

American Civil Liberties Union (ACLU)
125 Broad Street, 18th Floor
New York, NY 10004
(212) 549-2500
Web site: https://www.aclu.org
The ACLU is an organization that works in courts,
   legislatures, and communities to defend the rights
   and liberties granted in the U.S. Constitution and
   by law for every individual.

Department of Justice Canada
284 Wellington Street
Ottawa, ON K1A 0H8
Canada
(613) 957-4222
Web site: http://www.justice.gc.ca
The Department of Justice Canada supports the min-
   ister of justice by providing legal services to
   government and client departments. It also encourages respect for the rights and freedoms granted by
   the Constitution and the laws.

Lambda Legal
National Headquarters
120 Wall Street, 19th Floor
New York, NY 10005-3904

(212) 809-8585

Web site: http://www.lambdalegal.org

This national organization strives for full recognition of civil rights for lesbians, gay men, bisexuals, transgender people, and people with HIV.

National Organization for Marriage (NOM)

2029 K Street NW, Suite 300

Washington, DC 20006

(888) 894-3604

Web site: http://www.nationformarriage.org

NOM's mission statement includes protecting traditional marriage and the faith-based communities that encourage them.

Supreme Court of Canada

301 Wellington Street

Ottawa, ON K1A 0J1

Canada

(613) 995-4330 or 1 (888) 551-1185

Web site: http://www.scc-csc.gc.ca

The Supreme Court of Canada is the highest judicial court in Canada.

Supreme Court of the United States

1 First Street NE

Washington, DC 20543

(202) 479-3000

Web site: http://www.supremecourt.gov

The U.S. Supreme Court is the highest judicial court in the United States.

U.S. Department of Justice

950 Pennsylvania Avenue NW

Washington, DC 20530-0001

(202) 514-2000

Web site: http://www.justice.gov

The U.S. Department of Justice enforces the law, ensures public safety, federally engages in crime control, and pursues punishment for people who break laws.

WEB SITES

Due to the changing nature of Internet links, Rosen Publishing has developed an online list of Web sites related to the subject of this book. This site is updated regularly. Please use this link to access the list:

http://www.rosenlinks.com/UUSC/Marr

FOR FURTHER READING

Ayers, Tess, and Paul Brown. *The Essential Guide to Gay and Lesbian Weddings*. New York, NY: Experiment, 2012.

Badgett, M. V. *When Gay People Get Married: What Happens When Societies Legalize Same-Sex Marriage*. New York, NY: New York University Press, 2009.

Ball, Carlos A. *The Right to Be Parents: LGBT Families and the Transformation of Parenthood*. New York, NY: New York University Press, 2012.

Cahill, Sean, and Jason Cianciotto. *LGBT Youth in America's Schools*. Ann Arbor, MI: University of Michigan, 2012.

Catholic Answers. *Why Homosexual Unions Are Not Marriages*. Seattle, WA: Amazon Digital Services, 2012.

Clifford, Denis, Emily Doskow, and Frederick Hertz. *A Legal Guide for Lesbian & Gay Couples*. Berkley, CA: Nolo, 2010.

Corvino, John, and Maggie Gallagher. *Debating Same-Sex Marriage*. New York, NY: Oxford University Press, 2012.

Derfner, Joel. *Lawfully Wedded Husband: How My Gay Marriage Will Save the American Family*. Madison, WI: University of Wisconsin, 2013.

DeWitt, Peter M. *Dignity for All: Safeguarding LGBT Students*. Thousand Oaks, CA: Corwin, 2012.

Doskow, Emily, and Frederick Hertz. *Making It Legal: A Guide to Same-Sex Marriage, Domestic Partnership & Civil Unions*. Berkley, CA: Nolo, 2011.

Estes, Steve. *Ask and Tell: Gay and Lesbian Veterans Speak Out*. Chapel Hill, NC: University of North Carolina Press, 2008.

Klarman, Michael J. *From the Closet to the Altar: Courts, Backlash, and the Struggle for Same-Sex Marriage*. New York, NY: Oxford University Press, 2013.

Knox, David, and Caroline Schacht. *Choices in Relationships: An Introduction to Marriage and the Family*. Belmont, CA: Wadsworth, 2013.

Liptak, Adam. *To Have and Uphold the Supreme Court and the Battle for Same-Sex Marriage*. New York, NY: Byliner, Inc., 2013.

Parr, Todd. *The Family Book*. New York, NY: Little, Brown, 2010.

Pierceson, Jason. *Same-Sex Marriage in the United States: The Road to the Supreme Court*. Lanham, MD: Rowman & Littlefield, 2013.

Robinson, Gene. *G-d Believes in Love: Straight Talk About Gay Marriage*. New York, NY: Vintage Books, 2012.

Stone, Amy L. *Gay Rights at the Ballot Box*.
Minneapolis, MN: University of Minnesota, 2012.

Streitmatter, Rodger. *Outlaw Marriages: The Hidden Histories of Fifteen Extraordinary Same-Sex Couples*. Boston, MA: Beacon, 2012.

ViewCaps. *Gay Marriage*. Anaheim, CA: BookCaps Study Guides, 2013.

BIBLIOGRAPHY

Beckwith, Francis J. "Interracial Marriage and Same-Sex Marriage." Witherspoon Institute, May 21, 2010. Retrieved September 2013 (http://www .thepublicdiscourse.com/2010/05/1324).

Bill of Rights Institute. "*Loving v. Virginia* (1967)." 2010. Retrieved September 2013 (http:// billofrightsinstitute.org/resources/educator-resources/ lessons-plans/landmark-cases-and-the-constitution/ loving-v-virginia-1967).

Bio.true story. "Harvey Milk." Retrieved September 2013 (http://www.biography.com/people/ harvey-milk-9408170?page=2).

Brogan-Kator, Denise. "Federal Tax Equality." Family Equality Council, August 30, 2013. Retrieved September 2013 (http://www.familyequality.org/ equal_family_blog/2013/08/30/1719/ federal_tax_equality).

Burrelli, David F. "'Don't Ask, Don't Tell:' The Law and Military Policy on Same-Sex Behavior." Congressional Research Service, March 25, 2010. Retrieved September 2013 (http://digitalcommons .ilr.cornell.edu/key_workplace/727).

CNN. "Same-Sex Couples Ready to Make History in Massachusetts." May 17, 2004. Retrieved September 2013 (http://www.cnn.com/2004/ LAW/05/17/mass.gay.marriage).

CNN. "Vatican Fights Gay Marriage." CNN.com
World, July 31, 2003. Retrieved September 2013
(http://www.cnn.com/2003/WORLD/europe/07/31/
vatican.gay.marriages).

Cornell University Law School Legal Information
Institute. "*Lawrence v. Texas* (02-102) 539 U.S.
558 (2003) 41 S. W. 3d 349, Reversed and
Remanded." June 26, 2003. Retrieved September
2013 (http://www.law.cornell.edu/supct/html/02
-102.ZD.html).

Culhane, John. "The Most Ingenious Attack on Gay
Marriage Bans." *Slate*, October 2, 2013. Retrieved
September 2013 (http://www.slate.com/articles/
news_and_politics/jurisprudence/2013/10/the_
pennsylvania_lawsuit_with_the_best_chance_of_
toppling_state_laws_against.html).

DeSantis, Matthew, Jason Kessel, and Daniel A. Smith.
"Same-Sex Marriage Ballot Measures and the
2004 Presidential Election." State and Local
Government Review. Retrieved September 2013
(http://www.clas.ufl.edu/users/dasmith/SLGR2006
.pdf).

Doskow, Emily. "Recognition of Same-Sex
Relationships in Other States." Nolo.com, July 3,
2013. Retrieved September 2013 (http://www.
nolo.com/legal-encyclopedia/same-sex-marriage
-developments-law-29828-2.html).

Faith in America. "The Damaging Practice of Conversion or Reparative Therapy." Retrieved September 2013 (http://www.faithinamerica.org/reparative-therapy).

The Free Dictionary. "Constitutional Amendment." Retrieved September 2013 (http://legal-dictionary.thefreedictionary.com/Constitutional+Amendment).

Freedom to Marry. "The DOMA Legal Challenges." Retrieved September 2013 (http://www.freedomto-marry.org/pages/the-doma-legal-challenges).

Freedom to Marry. "The Freedom to Marry Internationally." Retrieved September 2013 (http://www.freedomtomarry.org/landscape/entry/c/international).

Garamone, Jim. "'Don't Ask, Don't Tell' Repeal Certified by President Obama." U.S. Department of Defense, July 22, 2011. Retrieved September 2013 (http://www.defense.gov/news/newsarticle.aspx?id=64780).

Greenhouse, Linda. "The Supreme Court: Homosexual Rights; Justics, 6–3, Legalize Gay Sexual Conduct in Sweeping Reversal of Court's '86 Ruling." *New York Times*, June 27, 2003. Retrieved September 2013 (http://www.nytimes.com/2003/06/27/us/supreme-court-homosexual-rights-justices-6-3-legalize-gay-sexual-conduct.html?pagewanted=all&src=pm).

Huffington Post. "Defense of Marriage Act Ruling Made by Supreme Court (FULL TEXT)." June 26, 2013. Retrieved September 2013(http://www .huffingtonpost.com/2013/06/26/defense-of -marriage-act-ruling_n_3454858.html).

Huffington Post. "Proposition 8 Timeline: A History of California's Gay Marriage Ban and Its Legal Challenges." June 26, 2013. Retrieved September 2013 (http://www.huffingtonpost.com/2013/06/ 26/proposition-8-timeline_n_3503512.html).

Human Rights Campaign. "The Lies and Dangers of Efforts to Change Sexual Orientation or Gender Identity." Retrieved September 2013 (http://www .hrc.org/resources/entry/the-lies-and-dangers -of-reparative-therapy).

Human Rights Campaign. "Respect for Marriage Act." July 30, 2013. Retrieved September 2013 (http://www.hrc.org/laws-and-legislation/federal -legislation/respect-for-marriage-act).

Infoplease. "The American Gay Rights Movement: A Timeline." 2013. Retrieved September 2013 (http:// www.infoplease.com/ipa/A0761909.html).

Jackson, David. "Obama Hails Court Decision Striking Down DOMA." *USA Today*, June 26, 2013. Retrieved September 2013 (http://www.usatoday. com/story/theoval/2013/06/26/obama-supreme-court -defense-of-marriage-act/2459427).

Kessler, Robert. "Only 14 of Last Year's 101 Major Studio Movies Had an LGBT Character." August 2013. Retrieved September 2013 (http://www.cele-buzz.com/2013-08-21/glaad-study-lgbt-characters-in-film).

Kilday, Gregg. "GLAAD Unveils First Studio Ranking of Gay Characters in Film." August 21, 2013. Retrieved September 2013 (http://www.holly-woodreporter.com/news/glaad-unveils-first-studio-ranking-609785).

Lambda Legal. Various pages. Retrieved September 2013 (http://www.lambdalegal.org).

Leitsinger. Miranda. "'*I Cried, I Cried*': DOMA Widow Says on Hearing of Supreme Court Win." NBC News, June 26, 2013. Retrieved September 2013 (http://usnews.nbcnews.com/_news/2013/06/26/19155699-i-cried-i-cried-doma-widow-says-on-hearing-of-supreme-court-win?lite).

Liptak, Adam. "Exhibit A for a Major Shift: Justices' Gay Clerks." *New York Times*, June 8, 2013. Retrieved September 2013 (http://www.nytimes.com/2013/06/09/us/exhibit-a-for-a-major-shift-justices-gay-clerks.html?pagewanted=all&_r=0).

Livio, Susan K. "NJ Gay Conversion Therapy Ban for Kids Challenged by Therapist Groups." *Star Ledger*, August 23, 2013. Retrieved September

2013 (http://www.nj.com/politics/index.
ssf/2013/08/nj_gay_conversion_therapy_ban_for_
kids_challenged_by_therapist_groups.html).

Majors, Steve. "Voices of Children." Family
Equality Council, March 5, 2013. Retrieved
September 2013 (http://www.familyequality.org/
equal_family_blog/2013/03/05/1567/
voices_of_children).

Merriam-Webster Online Dictionary and Thesaurus.
"Marriage." Retrieved September 2013 (http://
www.merriam-webster.com/dictionary/marriage).

Minnesota State Legislature. "1970 *Baker v. Nelson.*"
Retrieved September 2013 (http://www.leg.state
.mn.us/webcontent/lrl/issues/SameSexMarriages/
BakerNelson.pdf).

Mintz, Howard. "California Gay Conversion
Therapy Ban Upheld." *San Jose Mercury News,*
August 29, 2013. Retrieved September 2013
(http://www.mercurynews.com/crime-courts/
ci_23973557/california-gay-conversion-therapy
-ban-upheld).

Muller, Sarah. "MSNBC's Macklemore and Ryan
Lewis' Gay Rights Anthem 'Same Love' Wins at
MTV VMAs." MSNBC, August 26, 2013.
Retrieved September 2013 (http://tv.msnbc
.com/2013/08/26/macklemore-and-ryan-lewis-gay
-rights-anthem-same-love-wins-at-mtv-vmas).

National Archives and Records Administration. "The Bill of Rights." Retrieved September 2013 (http://www.archives.gov/exhibits/charters/bill_of_rights_transcript.html).

Newbeck, Phyl. "*Loving v. Virginia* (1967)." *Encyclopedia Virginia*, April 3, 2012. Retrieved September 2013 (http://www.encyclopediavirginia.org/Loving_v_Virginia_1967#start_entry).

Nichols, James. "Gay Military Couple on Spousal Benefits for Same-Sex Partners After 'Don't Ask, Don't Tell' Repeal." *Huffington Post*, September 26, 2013. Retrieved September 2013 (http://www.huffingtonpost.com/2013/09/26/military-same-sex-benefits_n_3996163.html#slide=1515593).

Nolo. "Recognition of Same-Sex Relationships in Other States." Retrieved September 2013 (http://www.nolo.com/legal-encyclopedia/same-sex-marriage-developments-law-29828-2.html).

Out Music. "A Brief History of 'Same Love.'" Retrieved September 2013 (http://www.out.com/entertainment/music/2013/08/27/brief-history-same-love#slide-3).

OutServe SLDN. "About 'Don't Ask, Don't Tell.'" Retrieved September 2013 (http://www.sldn.org/pages/about-dadt).

Pentin, Edward. "Vatican's Top American: DOMA Decision Will Lead to Deaths." Newsmax, July 2,

2013. Retrieved September 2013 (http://www
.newsmax.com/Newsfront/vatican-doma-decision
-deaths/2013/07/02/id/512964).

Pew Research Religion & Public Life Project. "Gay
Marriage Around the World." July 16, 2013.
Retrieved September 2013 (http://www.pewforum
.org/2013/07/16/gay-marriage-around-the
-world-2013).

Pilkington, Ed. "Elena Kagan Appointed to the
Supreme Court After US Senate Vote." *Guardian*,
August 5, 2010. Retrieved September 2013 (http://
www.theguardian.com/law/2010/aug/05/elena
-kagan-us-supreme-court).

ProCon.org. "14 States with Legal Gay Marriage and 35
States with Same-Sex Marriage Bans." September 27,
2013. Retrieved September 2013 (http://gaymarriage
.procon.org/view.resource.php?resourceID=004857).

Protect Marriage. Retrieved September 2013 (http://
protectmarriage.com).

Reilly, Mollie. "Michele Bachmann: DOMA,
Proposition 8 Rulings 'Attacked Our
Constitution.'" *Huffington Post*, June 26, 2013.
Retrieved September 2013 (http://www.huffington-
post.com/2013/06/26/michele-bachmann-doma
_n_3504640.html).

Reilly, Ryan J., and Sabrina Siddiqui. "Supreme Court
DOMA Decision Rules Federal Same-Sex

Marriage Ban Unconstitutional." *Huffington Post*, June 26, 2013. Retrieved September 2013 (http://www.huffingtonpost.com/2013/06/26/supreme-court-doma-decision_n_3454811.html).

Reuters. "Victory! Proposition 8 Is Unconstitutional for Good: Marriage Equality Returns to California." Reuters, June 26, 2013. Retrieved September 2013 (http://www.reuters.com/article/2013/06/26/dc-afer-prop-idUSnPNLA39021+1e0+PRN20130626).

Ridge, Hannah. "Gay Marriage 2013: Who Are the 26% of Young People Against Gay Marriage?" Policymic, March 2013. Retrieved September 2013 (http://www.policymic.com/articles/30570/gay-marriage-2013-who-are-the-26-of-young-people-against-gay-marriage).

Schwartz, John. "Judge Rules That Military Policy Violates Rights of Gays." *New York Times*, September 9, 2010. Retrieved September 2013 (http://www.nytimes.com/2010/09/10/us/10gays.html?_r=0).

Sims, Brian K. "Sims, Mullery to Introduce Ban on Anti-Gay 'Conversion Therapy' for Minors." Pennsylvania House of Representatives. Retrieved September 2013 (http://www.pahouse.com/Sims/index.asp?pg=PAHouseNews&doc=30194).

Southern Poverty Law Center. "Conversion Therapy." 2013. Retrieved September 2013 (http://www.splcenter.org/conversion-therapy).

Sullivan, Sean. "Public Wants Constitution to Decide Same-Sex Marriage." *Washington Post*, April 4, 2013. Retrieved September 2013 (http://www .washingtonpost.com/blogs/the-fix/wp/2013/04/04/ public-wants-constitution-to-decide-same-sex -marriage-not-states).

U.S. Department of Defense. "Don't Ask, Don't Tell Is Repealed." Retrieved September 2013 (http://www .defense.gov/home/features/2010/0610_dadt).

Von Drehle, David. "How Gay Marriage Won." *Time*, March 28, 2013. Retrieved September 2013 (http://swampland.time.com/2013/03/28/ how-gay-marriage-won).

INDEX

ABOUT THE AUTHOR

Barbara Gottfried Hollander has authored numerous books. She was an editor of the *New York Times* best seller *The World Almanac and Book of Facts*, and an author with the Council for Economic Education. Hollander received her B.A. in economics from the University of Michigan and her M.A. in economics from New York University. She serves on Rosen Publishing's Teen Health and Wellness Expert Review Board and the Literacy Connections Committee, which promotes literacy in special needs schools.

PHOTO CREDITS